WELCOME TO THE WORLD OF

Foxes

Diane Swanson

Whitecap Books
Vancouver / Toronto

Edited by Elizabeth McLean
Cover design by Steve Penner
Cover photograph by Tim Christie
Interior design by Margaret Ng
Typeset by Tanya Lloyd
Photo credits: John Sylvester/First Light iv, 24; Wayne Lynch 2, 10, 22, 26;
Herbert Lange/First Light 4; Brian Milne/First Light 6; Tim Christie 8, 16, 20;
Thomas Kitchin/First Light 12; Lynn M. Stone 14; Aubrey Lang 18

Printed and bound in Canada

Canadian Cataloguing in Publication Data

Swanson, Diane, 1944–
   Welcome to the world of foxes

   Includes index.
   ISBN 1-55110-705-8

   1. Foxes—North America—Juvenile literature. I. Title.
QL737.C22S92 1998   j599.775   C98-910011-1

For more information on
this series and other
Whitecap Books titles,
visit our web site at
www.whitecap.ca

The publisher acknowledges the support of the Canada Council for the Arts for
our publishing program and the Cultural Services Branch of the Government of
British Columbia in making this publication possible.

The author acknowledges Matt Austin of the Ministry of Environment, Lands
and Parks in British Columbia for reviewing this manuscript.

Contents

World of Difference

FURRY AND BUSHY-TAILED, FOXES ARE HANDSOME DOGS. They are cousins of the wolf—just as wild, but smaller. Five large foxes weigh less than one large wolf.

Around the world, there are about 20 different kinds of foxes. In North America, there are 4 main kinds, each with perky ears, a pointed snout, and a long tail.

The biggest—and most common—are red foxes, which aren't always red. Some are gray-brown or silvery black, but most have black legs and white-tipped tails.

Next in size are gray foxes with salt-and-pepper topcoats and black-tipped tails.

Taking life easy, this red fox rests its head on a bed of grass.

1

Muffled in fluffy fur, an Arctic fox sleeps warmly in freezing weather.

To spot a gray fox, you might have to look up. Long claws on their back feet help them climb trees.

Smaller Arctic foxes are usually white in winter to blend with the snow, but some are ice blue. In summer, their coats turn brown to blend with the ground. Arctic foxes have smaller ears and shorter legs than other foxes. That means less body heat escapes from these exposed parts. Fur on the soles of their feet helps keep them warm and makes it easier to walk on slippery ice.

North America's smallest foxes are the size of large house cats, and they're mostly gray in color. They have four main names: swift, kit, desert, and prairie fox. The first name comes from the speed they use to chase jackrabbits. Swift foxes can run faster than cars usually drive in cities.

When does a dog look and act like a cat? When the dog is a fox! It peers at the world through bright cat eyes with narrow, upright pupils. It creeps low like a cat, placing its back feet carefully where its front feet have just been. It twitches its tail, then springs into the air, and lands lightly—just like a cat. But all that's not too surprising. A fox and a cat need many of the same skills: they're both master mouse-catchers.

Where in the World

FOXES LIVE ALMOST EVERYWHERE—from seashores to forests, from deserts to frozen lands. Some make homes in the quiet of the wilderness. Others live in the bustle of the big city.

The Arctic fox lives in countries all around the Arctic Ocean. Its thick coat keeps it warm, especially when it curls up as a furry ball. The fox usually hunts along coasts and on thick ice that covers parts of the ocean in winter. If it must, it will travel long distances for food. Some Arctic foxes have traveled more than 2000 kilometres (1250 miles) to new hunting grounds.

To escape enemies, a sure-footed gray fox pup climbs a tree.

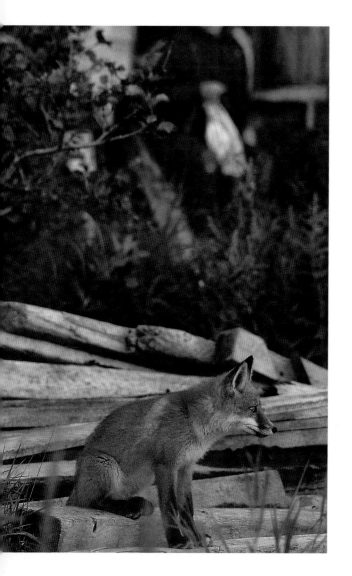

Except for thick woods and deserts, the red fox lives across Canada, the United States, Europe, Asia, Australia, New Zealand, and part of North Africa. It's so adaptable that it has even spread into the Arctic wilderness. It has also learned how to live close to people on farms and in towns.

The gray fox is adaptable,

For this red fox pup, the city is the place to live. Traffic is the greatest danger it faces.

too. But because it's a climber, it prefers to make its home in the woods. There, it leaps from tree to tree and runs along thick branches. The gray fox lives in the United States, Mexico, Central America, and parts of Canada and South America.

The dry lands of the western United States are home to the swift fox. It is also living in parts of southern Canada again. Like the gray and Arctic foxes, the swift fox lives in fewer places than it once did.

Out on the Town

When red foxes come to the city, they make themselves at home on golf courses, at cemeteries, and in parks. But one fox was recently found where none had been seen before. It was running among the busy crowds and bright lights of a huge, downtown shopping center.

No one knows how the fox got there, but all the excitement must have worn it out. When it was moved to a quiet wildlife shelter, it slept for most of a week.

World Full of Food

"Got it," this red fox pup seems to say, planting its paws firmly on a pheasant.

LISTENING, SMELLING, THE FOX IS ON THE HUNT. It can hear the footsteps of a beetle walking in the grass. It can sniff the scent of a rabbit, hours after one has hopped by.

The fox sees well, too, but it hunts mostly at night, depending more on its ears and nose. It often hunts small animals, such as mice and insects, but it's not fussy. It eats nearly anything it finds, including eggs, nuts, and grass. When it finds more than it can eat, it buries some for later.

In cities, the red fox adds pet food and compost to its menu. It raids garbage cans

9

Leap. Pounce. This Arctic fox is hunting a lemming it smells under the snow.

for popcorn and bits of pizza. It steals blueberries and other food from gardens. Stepping lightly across freshly watered lawns, it sniffs and listens for earthworms that have left their burrows. In one night, it might swallow 150 wriggling worms.

The swift fox hunts fast-running rabbits, but it also makes meals of tiny animals.

It gobbles up masses of grasshoppers in the summer. The gray fox, however, prefers to dine heavily on summer's wealth of plants.

The Arctic fox often hunts mouselike animals called lemmings. In winter, it sniffs them in their tunnels under the snow. Then it dives in, feet first, to catch them.

Sometimes the Arctic fox also eats leftovers from another animal's meal. It may even follow a hunting polar bear, then wait around for any scraps.

TO CATCH A MOUSE

The patter of tiny feet in the grass stops a fox in its tracks. Silent and still, it sniffs and waits to hear the patter again. Then it creeps s-l-o-w-l-y toward the sound.

As the fox gets close, the patter stops. But the fox is quick to pounce. Leaping up and forward on its strong back legs, it lands—front legs first. Pushing its paws through the grass, the fox traps the mouse, then chomps down. Dinner is served!

World of Words

FOXES GROWL AND FOXES HOWL. They talk like pet dogs, using many of the same sounds and actions.

Because foxes spend a lot of time alone, they often make long-distance calls to each other. One fox might scream, "Waaaah," especially at mating times, or it might cry out: "Wow, wow, wow." From far away, another fox might answer: "Wow, wow, wow."

Back and forth the foxes call as they gradually move nearer. When they get close, their doglike calls might change to chickenlike cluckings. The weaker fox

A red fox may say hello to other foxes by SCREAMING.

A snuggle is a warm greeting in any language — including Arctic fox talk.

might welcome the other with a high whine.

Then the foxes might let their bodies do the talking. If they're happy, they show it by wagging their tails. But if one fox wants to fight, it arches its back and snarls. The other fox might respond the same way, or it might press its body to the ground.

That's fox talk for, "I don't want to fight."

Like newborn dogs, new-born foxes whine for attention. The whines turn to barks as the pups grow older, and if they need help, they yelp. But when pups just want to say they're contented, they make a soft, trilling sound.

A parent fox "huffs" to welcome its pups and coughs to warn them of danger. If the pups are not close by, the parent barks instead. The pups don't waste time answering. They just leap for safety.

SMELL ME A STORY

A fox talks through smells. It sprinkles urine near its den to say, "This place is mine." Sometimes it sprays urine where it has stored food—after it eats the food. That's a smelly reminder that the "cupboard" is now empty.

When it waves its tail, a fox releases perfume from a small tail gland. Sometimes the perfume smells like violets. Scientists aren't sure exactly what the smell is saying, but foxes share it most often at mating times.

New World

NEWBORN FOXES LOOK NOTHING LIKE THEIR PARENTS. They don't have pointed fox faces; instead, their snouts are short and rounded. And the color of their fur is usually quite different from the adults' fur. Red foxes may be born with wooly brown coats; gray foxes, with black ones.

The number of newborns in a fox family varies a lot, but it's often four to six. As you might expect, the pups are very small. At birth, the largest kind of fox—the red—weighs only as much as a lemon.

A mother fox finds a safe, dry den to give birth to her pups. It may be a hollow

Red fox pups emerge from a den that they may share with another fox family.

17

From its cozy underground burrow, a gray fox peeks out at the world.

log or an empty cave. It may be a tunnel she digs herself or a burrow that was dug by some other animal. The climbing gray fox may pick a spot high up in a hollow tree.

Whatever den she chooses, the mother fox usually returns to the same one each year. But before she has more pups, she may work to make her home bigger and better.

At birth, the tiny fox pups snuggle helplessly together. They can't hear, and they can't see. Their mother stays with them day and night, keeping them safe, warm, and clean. She feeds the hungry pups her rich milk. The father fox hunts for food to feed her, delivering it right to the den.

After a few weeks, the fox pups are able to pop in and out of the den. They spend most of their time playing, eating, and sleeping—all under the watchful eyes of their parents.

AT HOME IN THE ARCTIC

It's hard to dig dens where much of the ground is frozen all year. Arctic foxes search riverbanks and hills for sandy soil that they can burrow into. But they may have to use a rock pile for a home.

Underground Arctic dens are usually sets of tunnels with 4 to 12 openings. Huge dens may have 100 openings. The dens are easy to spot because the grass above them is so healthy. All that digging by the foxes helps it grow.

Small World

FOX PUPS CAN'T SPEND ALL DAY JUST BEING PUPPIES. They have to learn how to hunt, too. They watch their parents closely and try hard to imitate them.

A hunting lesson might begin with a parent bringing home a dead bird. The pup sniffs and rolls the bird across the ground. It sneaks up and pounces on the bird, then tosses it about. Finally, the pup might fight with another pup for the bird. In later lessons, the parents might bring home a bird that is not yet dead.

The pup is soon ready to follow its parents on hunting trips. It must learn what

When they're away from the den, red fox pups stay where it's safe—close to a parent.

21

A swift fox checks out its pups. Big ears and a black-tipped tail are common among these foxes.

to eat—and how to catch it. The pup usually starts to hunt by grabbing easy prey, such as slow-moving insects.

The fox pup also learns to sniff out food that its parents have stored. Just for practice, it digs up the food, then buries it again, patting the dirt back with its nose.

While the pup is busy learning, the

parents are busy guarding. Foxes not only watch for enemies on the ground, they keep an eye on the sky. A hungry hawk might swoop down and snatch up a pup. At the slightest signal from its parents, the pup shoots to safety. For a gray fox, that usually means heading up a tree.

A fox is often less than a year old when it starts out on its own. If it has learned its lessons well—and if it's lucky—it may live to be 10 years old.

On the Lookout

One day, a swift fox spotted a coyote lurking near its den. The fox knew that its family was in danger. It waited until the coyote had passed, then moved its pups to a new home—an empty badger burrow. The fox dug the burrow deeper, then added more escape holes. The family was safe—for now.

Foxes of every kind are always on the lookout for enemies. Besides coyotes, they fear wolves, eagles, and people.

Fun World

WRESTLING, ROMPING, EVEN SOMERSAULTING. Young foxes are peppy, playful pups.

One might creep through tall grass, then pounce on some make-believe prey. Or the pup might shadow a beetle or jump on a bone. It might toss a twig into the air, then spring up to catch it.

When the mother fox is resting, her pups might sneak up on her, as if they were stalking a mouse. Or they might hurl themselves across her back or scramble all over her. Whenever she's had enough, she just moves off.

Fox pups mostly play with other fox pups. Together, they bark and yip. They nibble each other's ears and tails. And they jump, roll, and wrestle where it's safe—close to the entrance of their den.

Before they eat, the pups often play tug-of-war, grabbing the same piece of food and p-u-l-l-ing. The winner eats the

A swift fox licks its lips and nose after downing food it grabbed in play.

prize. They play a similar game when one of them has a toy, such as an old bone or a pine cone. The other pups try to yank it away.

Races and chases are also good fox fun. If the pups try to stop fast, they may flip a few somersaults. But all that play is great exercise. It helps the pups grow strong and trains them to be hunters that are quick on their feet. And it tires them out, making them ready for sleep. Collapsing in one big pile, fox pups nestle down for a nap.

FASCINATING FOXES

Foxes have always fascinated people. Here are four reasons why:

- Red foxes learn to cross busy city streets when the traffic is lightest.
- Arctic foxes live through freezing temperatures as low as –60° Celsius (–76° Fahrenheit).
- Swift foxes survive hot desert days in dens 1 metre (3 feet) under-ground.
- Gray foxes grip floating logs firmly enough to "sail" to nearby islands.

Index